ALL MONTSERRAT

Text of Father Josep M. Soler i Canals, Abbot of Montserrat.
Captions, photographs: Editorial Escudo de Oro, S.A.

Photographs: Salvador Gonzàlez Solé, Marc Linares and
FISA-Escudo de Oro Photographic Archives.

Design, lay-out and printing, entirely created
by the technical department of
EDITORIAL ESCUDO DE ORO, S.A.

e-mail: editorial@eoro.com
http://www.eoro.com

Montserrat

Editorial Escudo de Oro, S.A.

In a corbel in the Gothic cloister (14th century), two angels support the coat of arms of Montserrat, featuring a mountain crossed by a saw.

"With a saw of gold, the angels hewed twisting hills to make a palace for you." These simple unaffected words from Virolai, by Jacint Verdaguer, express the wonder many people feel when contemplating the mountain of Montserrat, moved as they are by a millennium of devotion to the image of Our Lady.

The mountain, a symbol of the presence of the godhead in all religions, at Montserrat has been a place of Christian worship and the site of a Benedictine monastery since the eleventh century.

Mountain, Shrine, Monastery and place of discovery are the core elements that form the complex and surprising world of Montserrat.

View of the north face of Mount Montserrat.

A SURPRISING WORLD

Situated 38 kilometres from Barcelona, near the towns of Manresa and Igualada, the unusual and graceful massif of Montserrat rises in the centre of Catalonia to 1,236 metres above sea level at the highest point, the Pic de Sant Jeroni. The surprising and eye-catching shapes of the mountain came into being through the forces of geological change in the distant past.

At the beginning of the Tertiary period, in the Eocene epoch, a stretch of mountainous land, the so-called Balearic continent, occupied what is now the Mediterranean Sea between the Balearic Isles and the Principality. A large river ran through this area and out into the gulf which occupied the area of what is now the Ebre basin.

The slow action of geological disturbances caused the continent to sink and the deposit of sedimentary material emerged and rose to a significant height because of the depression of the surrounding land. This sedimentary material, consisting of pebbles, bonded together by hard natural limestone cement, sands and clays, formed the mountain of Montserrat. It measures 10 km in length and 5 km in width with an elliptical perimeter of some 25 kms.

The unmistakable appearance of this small mountainous group is the reason why its name, translated into English, is "the serrated mountain". Water, sun, rain, frost and wind have all patiently worked it to create a number of perspectives. The great wealth of vistas it offers has captivated the popular imagination and has inspired numerous writers. Goethe, moved

Overall view of the mountain from Pla del Fideué (Olesa de Montserrat).

"Els Flautats" (The Pipes). Practically all the peaks of Montserrat have names, given to them long ago by people from the surrounding villages and often referring to the shape the rocks suggest. That known as "Els Flautats" is so called because it resembles a group of organ pipes and because the wind, blowing through the fissures, seems to make music.

by his friend Humboldt's tale, wrote "man will find rest in no place except his own Montserrat", an expression which was glossed by a Catalan poet when he said "when I am pricked by the thorn of homesickness, I feel Montserrat within me".

The Montserrat which nature presents us is indeed spectacular and already a symbol of introspection, but the true significance of the mountain cannot be fully comprehended unless we consider its close ties with the people who have visited and lived on it over the centuries. The setting for a long and eventful past, Montserrat is tightly bound to the vicissitudes that have affected the Catalan lands and helps us to understand its cultural and religious significance for Catalonia up to the present day. Numerous archeological finds, especially of ceramics decorated with a variety of patterns, provide evidence of human presence on the mountain since the Neolithic period. This prehistoric culture, which dates back to around 3,000 years BC, is called "Montserratina" because of the specific loca-

"El Faraó" (The Pharaoh) and part of the "Frares encantats" (Enchanted Frays).

View of "Les Agulles" (The Needles) from Can Solà.

Overall view of the mountain, and Monistrol.

Upper station on the Sant Joan funicular railway.

Ruins of the Hermitage of Sant Jaume.

"Les Magdalenes" (The Magdalenes).

"La Gorra Marinera" (The Sea Cap).

*"La Momieta"
(The Little
Mummy),
"El Pebrot"
(The Pimento),
"El Sereno",
"El Pito del
Sereno" (The
Watchman
and The
Watchman's
Whistle) and
"la Quarta de
Trinitats" (The
Fourth of
Trinities).*

*"The Roca
foradada"
(The Pierced
Rock).*

"L'Aubarda castellana".

"El Cavall Bernat" (The Horse Bernard) and view of the Virgin that crowns this rock, one of the most popular in Montserrat as the largest and most highly stylised needles on the entire mountain.

13

West face of Sant Jeroni (1,236 m), the highest peak on the mountain.

"L'Ajaguda" (The Seated One).

Torrent del migdia (Midday Torrent). So called because it is exactly noon when the sun falls in the middle of this mountain stream.

tion and unusual nature of the finds. There are also traces of cultures such as the Bronze and Iron Ages, and the Monastery has pieces of flint, metal objects and human remains from the much later Iberian period. But it would be many years before the Montserrat of history began.

The text of a donation made by Wilfred the Hairy to the Pyrenean Monastery of Ripoll is the first written information we have. Wilfred, the first Count of Barcelona, had conquered the Arabs and taken the land around Montserrat between 875 and 876. Shortly afterwards, in 888, he donated a part of this conquered land with the four hermitages on it to Ripoll. Two of these hermitages, Sant Martí and Sant Per, were at the foot of the mountain and two were higher up on the mountain: Santa Maria, the origins of the current Basilica, and Sant Iscle, the only one which still exists today, built in what are now the Monastery gardens probably during the period of the Visigoths before the Arab invasion in 711. Thus began Montserrat's development.

South face, "La Salamandra" and, at the end, "El Camell d'Ecos" (The Camel of Echoes).

Montgrós is the largest rock in the entire range. Above, right, the so-called "La roca plana dels llamps" (The flat rock of lightning). ▷

"El Camell de Sant Jeroni" (Saint Jerome's Camel).

"The Bandereta" (The Pennant).

"The Portella Gran".

"The Bola de la Partió".

View of "Les Agulles", the needles, and partial views of this area: "El Bacallà" (the Cod) and "El Lloro" (The Parrot).

"La Boleta foradada"
(La Pierced Ball).

"La Nina" (The Doll) and
"El Dit" (The Finger).

"El Lloro", "La Monja" and "El Frare Gros" (The Fat Fray).

Zone around "Els Frares encantats".

Ruins of the Church of Sant Pau Vell.

THE MONASTERY IS BORN

The privileged site of the mountain, its steep rock formations and its silence soon attracted Christians, who led a life of prayer and penitence there. However, the flowering of Montserrat began with the fame acquired by the Hermitage of Santa Maria.

Ripoll was an influential centre concerned with other matters and scarcely paid any attention to its small distant churches on Montserrat. So, in the middle of the tenth century, the abbot of the Monastery of Santa Cecília, located on the mountain itself, claimed the property for himself until such time as it was reclaimed from him before the civil and religious authorities.

In 1008, Oliba, son of the count of Besalú and Cerdanya,

Oliba Cabreta, and great-grandson of Wilfred the Hairy, was elected as abbot of Ripoll. He recommended the dispute over the possession of the hermitages and surrounding lands on Montserrat and won them back for his Monastery. Oliba was one of the most important figures in Romanesque Catalonia. He was an advocate of the arts and literature and a careful writer, and turned Ripoll into an important religious and cultural centre. He was soon elected as abbot of Sant Miquel de Cuixà and shortly after that was named bishop of Vic. It was he who instituted the *Treva de Déu* (the Peace of God), which limits the length of struggles and combats. Once the hermitages on Montserrat had been regained, Oliba decided to establish a new monastery on the solitary mountain and installed a group of monks from Ripoll in the hermitage of Santa Maria. This was in 1025. The small Benedictine monastic community soon received visitors and pilgrims, who began to spread stories of the miracles and wonders worked there by Our Lady. These tales of extraordinary healings and grace, so much to the taste of the Middle Ages, brought increasing numbers of pilgrims and donations to the nascent priory. It soon became clear that the old chapel was too small and in the twelfth century a new one had to be built. The façade of this Romanesque chapel still remains in one of the side walls of the Basilica atrium.

The six "Canticles" dedicated by King Alphonse the Wise to Saint Mary of Montserrat are evidence of her growing fame and tell of many wonders and give thanks to Our Lady:

Mui grandes noit'e dia (Full many a long night and day
devemos dar porende day we must give thanks
nos a Sancte Maria thanks to Saint Mary,
graças, porque defende for she protects us
os seus de dano from danger and
et sen engano does not mislead but
en salvo os guia. guides us to safety).

HISTORICAL BACKGROUND

Starting in the thirteenth century, the character of Montserrat become more and more clearly defined. Rapid and vigorous growth has made it the most prestigious Shrine in Catalonia and one of the best-known throughout the Christian world. With the conquests of the Catalan-Aragonese crown, devotion to Our Lady of Montserrat spread eastwards to such an extent that the number of churches and chapels dedicated to her in the Italian regions reached 150. Her cult later spread into central Europe. The fame of Montserrat travelled to the west when the Americas were evangelised because of the early bonds created through the presence of a former monk from the mountain, Bernard Boïl, who was travelling with Christopher Columbus as the Papal Legate.

1409 was to be the most important year for the future of the Monastery; Benedict XIII decided to grant it independence from the abbey at Ripoll and the first abbot of Montserrat elected by the monks was Marc de Vilalba, a man of great diplomatic qualities who actively participated in the politics of the country. One of his successors, Antoni Pere Ferrer, continued this

Monastery of Santa Cecília.

Portal of the old Romanesque church (12th century).

of Ignatius of Loyola, and took effective charge of his monks' monastic and cultural life. In 1499 he brought the new art of printing to the Monastery by taking on the German master Johannes Luschner.

Hermitry, which had existed at Montserrat for many years and in all probability since before the founding of the Monastery, continued to flourish at that time and was to continue until the Napoleonic Wars. The life of work and prayer led by the hermits in their hermitages dotted around the mountains was governed by the Father Superior at the Monastery in accordance with established rules and customs.

The considerable activity at the Shrine clearly demonstrated the small size of the Romanesque church, a problem which was not resolved until Bartomeu Garriga was named abbot and in 1560 began the construction of the current church with loyal support from pilgrims and visitors. The work was finished in 1592.

The seventeenth century was a tumultuous and difficult period for Montserrat because of the wars, which laid the Principality to waste, and because of the heightened tension eventually caused by the new régime introduced by the monks from Valladolid. In 1641, when the uprising against the central authorities took place during the Reapers' War, the most important representative body in Catalonia, the Diputació del Govern General, took the monks imposed by the Castilian crown to the border. However, once the uprising had been quashed, Montserrat once again came under the control of Valladolid.

Montserrat was fortified twice when the French Wars broke out in spite of its poor suitability as a strategic site. In 1811 and 1812 Napoleon's army burnt it down and blew up the group of buildings, leaving the Shrine practically in ruins. The wealth of treasure donated during the previous centuries had been sold by the community to sustain resistance against the invaders. In 1812, only a pile of scorched stones and some half-destroyed buildings remained of the former Montserrat. Fortunately, the Image of Our Lady was saved as it had been hidden somewhere on the mountain.

During the troubled nineteenth century, Montserrat began the slow process of renewal and reconstruction against the background of the political struggles of the period. However, everything came to a halt with the 1835 Decree of Disentailment and the law on the dissolution of religious orders which meant the community had to leave the Monastery. When the monks returned in 1844, they came back to an enormous task fraught with difficulties and problems. In 1858 the

policy and took a strong position against John II in the civil war which started after the death of the prince of Viana.

However, these political struggles had a noticeable effect on the Monastery and made it difficult to lead a monastic life there, and so the need for reform began to be felt. In 1493 Ferdinand II, the Catholic Monarch, annexed Montserrat to the Congregation of San Benito el Real in Vallodolid and this entailed the arrival of Castilian monks who did not know the language and customs of the country. In spite of the difficulties caused by the royal imposition of reform (for example, Abbot Joan de Peralta was removed from the Monastery by being named bishop of Vic), the Monastery went through a period of regeneration under the direction of Abbot García de Cisneros, who was first cousin to the famous cardinal of the same name. Cisneros was a deeply religious man and a good organiser. He wrote the "Exercise of Spiritual Life", which was widely circulated and was highly influential on the writings

Cable car over the River Llobregat.

Archive image of the old funicular railway train.

which has become an exceptional means of access to the Sanctuary and an tourist attraction in itself.

Finally, during the course of the twentieth century, special mention must be made of Abbot Antoni M. Marcet, whose leadership brought about intense religious and cultural development within the community, with the establishment of the Monastery library and the First Liturgical Congress held in 1915 (with two further Congresses in 1965 and 1990), which led to a renewal in the liturgy in many areas of the Church in Catalonia. Improvements were also made during this period to the approaches to the Shrine with the installation of cable cars and funiculars.

The 1936 civil war caused little material damage to the Monastery as it had been seized by the government of the Generalitat de Catalunya, although twenty-three monks lost their lives. Once the civil war was over, the image of Our Lady was enthroned on its new throne in 1947, prompted by Abbot Aureli M. Escarré and supported by public contributions. Many people attended the celebrations, which were a popular cultural renewal of Catalonia after the war. Abbot Escarré continued in the direction taken by his predecessor, Abbot Marcet, and encouraged cultural flowering at the Monastery as well as developments in the liturgy and monastic life and physical improvements to the Shrine. His successors, Gabriel M. Brasó, Cassià M. Just and Sebastià M. Bardolet, have all continued the same policies while adapting them to new trends and concerns. During these last years stand out the attempts to restore the hermit way of living in the mountain, but without having achieved the continuity.

These features, which have marked the history of Montserrat, enable us to understand the direction that the Shrine and Monastery have taken up till now. Montserrat is a rich and varied setting that is at times disconcerting. It draws us not just with its natural or artistic riches but also with its religious and human background which is closely linked to the feelings of the people of Catalonia.

A group of Benedictine nuns settled in the former Monastery of Santa Cecília in 1952 and moved to the Monastery of Sant Benet in 1955, some four kilometres from the Marian Shrine, where they continue their life of prayer and receive pilgrims.

The two monasteries, the presence of hermits and the pilgrims make the mountain of Montserrat a place of worship and prayer to God, a place for deepening spiritual values and making supplications for the joys and troubles of all humanity.

Pope named Miquel Muntades abbot of Montserrat and, as the Congregation at Valladolid had disappeared, the Monastery became fully independent again and adhered to the Italian Congregation of Subiaco. Efforts to reconstruct the Shrine then increased. This reconstruction was to be very important for the people of Catalonia, closely linked as it was to the *Renaixença* (Renaissance: the literary, cultural and political rebirth of Catalonia) which made large groups of Catalans aware of their distinctive characteristics. This rapprochement of facts caused that, in 1880, the supposed millenarian of the discovery of the Sacred Image was celebrated and, the following year, the festivities surrounding the coronation of the image of Our Lady as patron saint of Catalonia as granted by Pope Leo XIII. In order to help pilgrims visiting the Monastery, the much-loved rack railway was built in 1892 and continued to run until 1957. In April 2003, using practically the same route but applying the present technology to the maximum, the new train was inaugurated

The new funicular railway to the sanctuary, opened in 2003.

Orella d'Ós (Ramonda Myconi).

Corona de Reina (Saxifaga cellosa subsp. catalaunica).

A LAND OF FANTASY: THE NATURAL PARK

The visual spectacle to be enjoyed in contemplating the mountain cannot be momentary or hurried. We need to be serene in order to be able to absorb all its beauty and to fix our eyes on the unusual rock formations and the harmony of the great wealth of vegetation.

Montserrat grows and transforms itself before our very eyes; it becomes alive, constantly changes colour, takes on new perspectives and its peaks, often surrounded by cloud, seem in our marvelling imagination to fly up to the sky. The shape of the mountain is so astonishing, so improbable, that it is unique throughout the world and might even make us think of the creative hand of an artist or child...

The fantastic shapes of the rocks and needles of Montserrat inspired people living long ago in nearby villages to give names to the most important formations - names as poetic or picturesque as "Els Frares encantats" (the enchanted monks), "El Camell" (the camel), "El Cap de mort" (Death's head), "Els flautats" (the flutes), "La Mòmia" (the mummy), "El Cavall Bernat" (Bernard the horse), "La Roca forada" (the pitted rock), "La Cadireta" (the small chair)... These people also wove strange tales around these rocks.

It is still surprising that such a rocky massif as this should have such exuberant vegetation in spite of the devastating fires in recent years. All around trees, bushes and plants cling to the rock itself in their eagerness for invincible life and beauty. These plants flourish in the favourable climactic conditions 1000 metres above sea level, in the shady damp ravines, in the sunny windblown rocky outcrops which offer rich soil to plant life (holm oaks, yews, pines, rosemary, heather, box trees etc.) and a favourable environment for a wide variety of animals (including wild boar, badgers, weasels, foxes and vipers, as well as the recently re-introduced goats), especially birds (eagles, ravens, owls, woodpigeons, blackbirds, etc.), and a large number of insect varieties. The interior of the rocks has also been worked by water and other agents. The caves of Salnitre in the area of Collbató were formed in this way. These caves, which are over 500 metres long, offer the visitor an astonishing journey amongst stalactites and stalagmites which are interesting from a scientific point of view and suggestive to the artistic mind. Some of the chasms are over a hundred metres in depth. There are grottoes, some of which were used in prehistoric times for dwellings and burial places, while others became shelters for hermits and there are many others which were the object of various popular stories. All this wealth and diversity produces a world of wonder, which, between the fable of the enchanted land and the material world of men and women today, lives and breathes in the very heart of Montserrat.

The mountain is a homogenous ensemble, geographically, geologically and geomorphically, which constitutes a special ecological unit within the natural environment of Catalonia with a unique richness, particularly as far as flora are concerned. The Patronat de la Muntanya de Montserrat (the Mountain of Montserrat Association) was founded in 1950 to ensure the conservation of this environment and in 1989, to widen this protection, the Parlament de Catalunya (the Parliament of Catalonia) created the Natural Park of the Mountain of Montserrat under the control of the Patronat.

Bonelli's eagles and goats.

THE "MORENETA"

History testifies that just after the current image of Saint Mary –Our Lady– was put in place in the Romanesque church, the number of the faithful and the fame of the Monastery grew progressively. At the beginning of the thirteenth century, James I was already talking of the small church of Montserrat as a place "which God embellishes and illustrates with continuous miracles". Precisely during those years, the Confraria (brotherhood) of devotees of Our Lady of Montserrat was established. This institution has, over the centuries, had many members who have spiritually adhered to the monastic community and have trusted to its prayer.

The "Moreneta", commonly so called because of the dark colour of her face, is a Romanesque wooden sculpture dating from the end of the twelfth or beginning of the thirteenth century. Restoration work was required on many subsequent occasions and particularly after the Napoleonic Wars of the nineteenth century. The image, a work of serene austere beauty, owes its colour to the slow change in the varnish (by a process of oxidation) on the face and hands caused by the passage of time and the effect of candle smoke and lamps burnt over many years in the small Romanesque church. For Christians familiar with the Scriptures, the Holy Image evokes the "spouse" of the book Song of Songs, "brown and beautiful" according to the Biblical author and to the Church liturgy.

Our Lady is crowned with a diadem and wears a headdress of many colours and a golden robe and cloak; she is sitting in a hieratic position and holds a ball in her left hand. The Child is sitting on her lap. He is crowned and clothed in a similar fashion and making a sign of blessing with His right hand while holding a pine cone in His left. The sculpture was moved from the Romanesque church to its current site in 1599. In 1881 she was crowned in accordance with canon law and proclaimed patron of the dioceses in Catalonia and in 1947 was placed upon her current throne.

This image of the Mother of Jesus has grown in importance over the course of the years and is the expression of a spiritual presence on Montserrat which makes her both venerable and attractive. The image represents one of central tenets of the Christian faith: the mystery of the Incarnation, of the Son of God made man in Jesus of Nazareth. Mary, with her son in her arms, reveals the love of God for man, to whom Jesus offers life and immortality through the Easter mystery of his death and resurrection. The mystery of the Incarnation, which culminates at Easter, sustains the universe created by God.

Image of Our Lady of Montserrat, "La Moreneta".

The Montserrat Boy's Choir.

THE CHOIR

There is already documentary evidence of the existence of the Montserrat Choir at the end of the thirteenth century. The Choir is a religious and musical institution made up of young boys. Whatever the date it started, it can be considered now as the oldest conservatoire in Europe. It probably originated from one of the "schools of psalm and song" which existed at the end of the twelfth century in the cathedrals and other churches in Catalonia, and has continued through to our times, reaching the high level of quality for which it is world famous. Over the centuries, the Choir has produced a number of choirmasters, organists and instrumentalists for the Church and has trained notable teachers and composers, particularly during the seventeenth and eighteenth centuries.

The Shrine has many features, of which the Choir is one of the most popular and charming, as demonstrated by the great number of visitors and pilgrims who attend the singing of the Salve Regina at midday. There are currently fifty choirboys, who receive an introduction to music in accordance with the ancient tradition of Montserrat. As well as voice training, solfeggio, polyphonic singing and gregorian chant, the boys receive a social, literary and scientific education and must also study a specific musical instrument, while the most gifted are instructed in the techniques of composing music. The choirboys take part in the prayers of the Shrine with the community of monks and continue, through their musical offering, the tradition of centuries.

The Montserrat Boy's Choir.

View of the main front and tower of the monastery from La Miranda de Fra Garí.

THE BASILICA

The uneven land on which the Shrine of Montserrat is built means that its construction is entirely irregular in shape. The group of buildings –built, destroyed and then reconstructed over the course of the years– consists of two large sections: the Basilica with monastic outbuildings and the buildings for accommodating and providing services for pilgrims and tourists. In artistic terms, the more interesting part by far is the Basilica and outbuildings.

The Atrium

At the end of the upper squares, the most notable feature is the robust shape of the west end of the Monastery with its tower that was constructed after the 1936-39 civil war. This entire architectural group reveals the char-

acter of its architect, Francesc Folguera. The three large balconies at the top are decorated with reliefs which, apart from the lower panels that form the lower part of the frame of the door to the central balcony, are the work of the sculptor Joan Rebull. In the lower part, below the arches, there are two sixteenth century tombs, the porch of the old Romanesque church (twelfth century) and a statue of Saint Benedict in wrought iron by Domènec Fita. Leaning against this façade are two wings from the Gothic cloister which was built in 1376 by the masters of Barcelona, Jaume Alfons and Pere Basset, on the orders of the abbot in commendam (who held the office in the absence of a regular incumbent and did not reside at Montserrat) of the time, Giuliano della Rovere, who was to be the future Pope Julius II, and whose shield decorates this lithe late-Gothic building.

The Gothic cloister has two storeys, the lower adorned with Gothic arches, the upper with carpanel, or three-centred arches.

Two capitals in the Gothic cloister. The first represents a man with the body of a fantastic animal, the second shows naked men and women dancing in a circle.

Between the arches in the Gothic cloister are inserted men's heads representing the different classes in society.

The atrium that provides access to the church is from the eighteenth century, although it did undergo some alterations in the middle of the twentieth century. Of particular note are the series of scratch-work and sculptures of saints or kings connected with Montserrat in its combined role of Benedictine Monastery and Marian Shrine. Images which stand out are those of St. John the Baptist and Saint Joseph sculpted by Josep Clarà. In this atrium is the baptistry with its door which has a representation of the cycle of Church sacraments according to the catechism beginning with baptism.

The so-called Gothic Chamber, adjoining the Gothic cloister, was reformed in 1955 using elements from earlier constructions, such as the arches and the corbels.

14th-century tombs of Joan of Aragon (left) and Bernat de Vilamarí, in the portal of the main front of the monastery.

Baptistery door in the basilica atrium. The sculptural reliefs are by the Swiss artist Charles Collet (1902-1983) and symbolise the salvation of the children of God in the Church.

Baptismal fount, in the Baptistery.

Atrium floor, designed by Father Benet Martínez. The medallion and the inscription around it reveal the symbolic message: only those baptised and born in the water like fish can understand the meaning of the fish of the Eucharist.

Sgrafitti decorating the walls of the porticoed section in the atrium.

The basilica façade, designed in neo-Plateresque style by Francesc de P. Villar Lozano, was built between 1900 and 1901. The sculptures of the Apostles are by Agapit Vallmitjana, whose brother Venanci produced the reliefs in the three tympanums.

Basilica: nave.

The Church

Abbot Bartomeu Garriga, as we have already seen, was responsible for the building of the Basilica of Montserrat in the sixteenth century. The works were carried out under the direction of Miquel Sastre and took thirty-two years to complete because of the magnitude of the project and the natural difficulties presented by the site. It was consecrated on 2 February 1592 and opened to the faithful. Leo XIII raised it to the status of basilica in 1881. The original plateresque façade was replaced between 1900 and 1901 by the current façade, which is the work of Francesc de P. Villar with sculptures by the brothers Venanci and Agàpit Vallmitjana.

The central aisle is 68.32 metres long, 21.5 wide and 33.33 high. In spite of the period when it was built, it is covered with very rounded Gothic arches which are firm-

Basilica: High Chapel.

43

The High Altar. The Christ presiding over the altar is an Italian work from the 16th century, whilst the cross support the figure, dating back to 1959, is by the silversmith Manuel Capdevila, who also created the baldachin that crowns it.

The altar front is decorated with fine enamels by Montserrat Mainar in 1958. The central panel represents the Last Supper, whilst on the right is the Miracle of the Bread and Fishes and on the left the Marriage of Canaan. At either end are two angels, one with the sacrificial bread, the other with a censer.

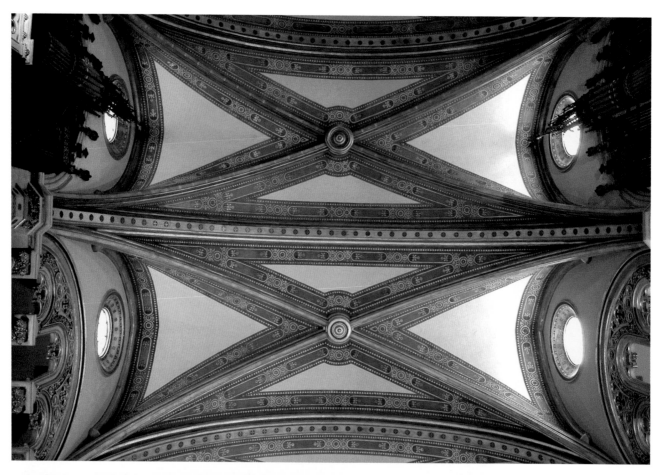

Detailed view of the vaults of the nave and the dome. The octagonal dome, though hinted at in the vault structures, was not built until the final restoration of the basilica, between 1991 and 1996.

The polychromed wood figures of the four major prophets in the buttresses of the nave were carved in 1896 by Josep Llimona.

The Altar of Sant Josep de Calassanç seen from the upper choir. Facing the grille are lamps that decorate the basilica, made to mark the occasion of the enthronement in 1947.

Sculpture of Saint Peter enthroned with the keys of the Church, by Josep Viladomat (1899-1989). The side chapels are all adorned by stained glass illustrating a scene from the life of Our Lady. That in the first chapel as we enter, on the right, represents the Presentation of the Child Jesus in the Temple.

Altar of Sant Ignasi de Loiola, built in 1893. The neo-Romanesque triptych, was designed by Francesc Rogent i Pedrosa, the paintings are by Ramir Lorenzale i Rogent and the sculpture of Pope Saint Clement is by Venanci Vallmitjana. The stained-glass window in this chapel depicts the Adoration of the Magi.

Altarpiece of Saint Martin, showing Saint Martin cutting his cloak in half to share it with a poor man. It was designed by Joan Riera, whilst the central sculpture is by Josep Llimona in 1896. The sculptures of Saint Placid and Saint Maur on the sides were added later.
The stained-glass window in this chapel depicts the Birth of Jesus.

Altar of Sant Josep de Calassanç (1891), a magnificent Catalan Modernist work by Francesc Berenguer i Mestres, a follower and collaborator of Gaudí, whose influence can be seen in various elements here. The stained-glass window in this chapel represents the Visitation.

Altar of La Immaculada, a beautiful Catalan Modernist work designed and directed by Josep M. Pericas in 1910. The altarpiece and figures are in white marble, whilst the two mosaic panels depict lilies against a gilt background. The decorative elements take their inspiration from plants, though we can also see strange forms evoking the ribcage of a palaeontological animal over each of the three figures.

The stained-glass in the Chapel of La Immaculada is different in conception from the others, as the window was not opened until 1910. In it, the artist Darius Vilàs produces an interesting effect by superimposing three layers of glass.

The second chapel on the left as we enter is that of El Sant Crist, and is presided over by a figure of Christ by Josep Llimona.
The stained-glass window in this chapel depicts the Flight into Egypt.

The Chapel of El Santíssim was renovated in 1977: the sculptural work is by Josep Maria Subirachs, the gold and silver work by Manuel Capdevila and the liturgical furnishing by Joaquim Capdevila. Despite the apparent austerity of the altar, it contains a rich iconographic programme: the altarpiece shows Christ Resuscitated, represented solely by His face in negative, His hands and feet marked by the nails and His side showing the spear wound, whilst the altar front is adorned by a bare femur symbolising death.

ly supported by the walls which separate the six side chapels. Together, they constitute an unusual building amongst the monuments of Catalonia and mark the transition from the Gothic to Renaissance. The interior of the church was restored with somewhat eclectic decoration following the destruction by Napoleon's armies. A programme of works was carried out between 1992 and 1996 to return the exterior to its original Renaissance design, which was lost due to various additions. The interior also underwent some restoration so that more light could enter through the reopening of the side windows and the octagonal dome to offset the shady colour the building had acquired over the course of time. All of this work was overseen by the architect Arcadi Pla.

The third chapel on the left as we enter is presided over by the painting of the "Flight into Egypt" by Josep Cusachs in 1904. The stained-glass window in this chapel represents the Child Jesus Lost in the Temple.

Chapel of Saint Scholastica, sister of Saint Benedict. The central sculpture is by Enric Clarasó. The stained-glass window in this chapel represents the Wedding in Canaan.

In the Middle Ages, pilgrims showed their devotion by hanging lamps in the former Church of Montserrat. This tradition was later revived and is still alive today.

Stained-glass window in the last chapel on the left as we enter, depicting Saint John the Evangelist taking Communion with Our Lady.

Stained-glass rose window in the basilica designed by Enric Montserdà and made at the Amigó brothers' workshop in 1894. It represents the Coronation of Our Lady. The crown is that donated by the Catalan people in 1881 to commemorate the proclamation of the virgin as the patron. Particularly magnificent features of this work are the colour range and the harmonious composition of the figures.

Chapel of Saint Benedict. Over the altar is the painting "Saint Benedict, Young Subiacan", by Montserrat Gudiol. The work was commissioned in 1980 to celebrate the 1,500th anniversary of the birth of Saint Benedict, founder of the Benedictine Order. The stained-glass window in this chapel represents the Annunciation.

Steps up to the Shrine and Angel Door, thus known due to the many angel musicians adorning it. Alabaster is used throughout, and the profuse sculptural decoration is by Enric Monjo between 1946 and 1954.

Stained-glass window in the last chapel on the right as we enter, representing the Marriage of Mary and Joseph.

Mosaics on the walls of the steps up to the Shrine. The saints depicted here allude to Mary's virginity and maternity: those on the left going up are mother saints, whilst those on the right are virgin saints. The mosaics were designed by Dom Benet M. Martínez and made by Santiago Padrós in 1947.

Along the length of the central aisle are numerous votive lamps of extraordinary gold-work, with some pieces of exceptional beauty. These lamps were offered by the cities and districts of Catalonia and by various groups and organisations. The statues of the prophets Ezekiel, Jeremiah, Isaiah and Daniel by Josep Llimona stand out amongst the central abutments. All four prophets speak about the arrival of the Messiah in their books and so occupy an important place in the Marian Basilica.

The most remarkable part of the interior is the Presbytery surrounded by three rows of neo-Gothic choir-stalls for the community of monks. The walls are decorated with a series of paintings by Joan Llimona, Baixeres, Graner and Riquer, which form a unique collection of *Modernista* Catalan paintings on a religious theme. In the centre, placed on some green marble steps, is the high altar –a block of stone weighing 8,000 kilos taken from the mountain itself– which has an antependium with enamels by Montserrat Mainar. Above the altar, hanging from the baldachin canopy, there is an ivory Christ figure, attributed to Ghiberti (sixteenth century), nailed to a cross decorated with Easter stories from the middle of the twentieth century.

To the right of the aisle is the chapel of the Holy Sacrament, which underwent changes in 1977 with sculptures by Subirachs and work by the Capdevila goldsmiths. Also of note are the chapels of Mary Immaculate (on the right-hand side), Sant Martí and Sant Josep de Calassanç in the *Modernista* style and of Saint Benedict with a painting by Montserrat Gudiol (on the left-hand side).

Three views of the anteroom on the right of the Niche, built in 1946 by the architect Francesc Folguera. The murals are by Josep Obiols, who also designed the silver doors. The sculpture of the choirboy is by Margarida Sans Jordi (1954).

The Niche

The wide marble staircase which leads to the Niche, located at the back of the church, opens out into a carved alabaster doorway by Enric Monjo with Marian stories and flanked by two candelabra that are also made of alabaster by Rafael Solanich. The interior of the stairway is decorated with beautifully-made mosaics designed by Fr. Benet Martínez, one of the monks of Montserrat. The two antechambers to the throne of the Holy Image contain paintings by Josep Obiols. Two pairs of beaten silver doors lead to the small throne room, visible from the central aisle. The dome and walls of the throne room are decorated with golden mosaics designed by Obiols, which show Our Lady of Montserrat being proclaimed patron saint of Catalonia and other Marian scenes. There are nine worked sil-

Vault in the throne room. The central medallion in the mosaic represents the right hand of God, with a dove (symbolising the Holy Spirit) just over the figure of Jesus, or the Son, sitting in the Virgin's lap. All the mosaics in this room were designed by Josep Obiols and produced by Santiago Padrós in 1947.

ver lamps, representing the eight Catalan dioceses and the Community of Montserrat, around the room. Reliefs by Joaquim Ros representing the Nativity and the Visitation of Mary flank the throne. Above the Image there are reproductions of the crown, sceptre and lily offered by the people of Catalonia to Our Lady (the originals are kept in the museum).

The back part of this room leads to the circular niche built between 1876 and 1884 by Villar i Carmona in a pre-*Modernista* style with Gothic and Romanesque features. The famous architect Gaudí played an important role in the direction of this work. The vault is decorated with frescos by Joan Llimona, which show

The throne area, seen from the basilica nave.

The throne of Our Lady of Montserrat was made in 1947, funded by a popular collection all over Catalonia. It was designed as a triptych by the architect Francesc Folguera. The reliefs flanking the image of the Virgin, by Joaquim Ros, represent the Nativity and the Visitation of Mary.

Two views of the Niche, or Cambril, a room built between 1876 and 1887. Between the arches are sculptures of angels. Image of Saint George, by Agapit Vallmitjana in 1893, behind which is the stained-glass window designed by the architect F. Villar Carmona and made by Antoni Rigalt. It depicts two groups of angels carrying Our Lady of Montserrat the insignia for Her coronation as patron saint of Catalonia (1881): the crown and the sceptre.

the pilgrims of Montserrat being received by Saint Mary.

The exit from the niche is via the Path of the Ave Maria, where pilgrims leave the candles they offer to Our Lady as an act of thanks or in remembrance of the prayer they have said at the Shrine. The route is decorated by a series of pieces of majolica which have Marian invocations on them. A piece of sculpture by Apel.les Fenosa evokes the angel of the Annunciation to Mary.

Path of Ave María.

The Altar of the Cambril or Niche is decorated by a mosaic depicting Christ crowning His mother.

The sacristy: overall view general and partial view of the cross which hangs from the ceiling.

The New Sacristy

The new Sacristy was built by the architect Francesc Folguera and consists of a vestibule, a spacious room with cupboards and a small apse. In the vestibule there is the tomb and statue in bronze by Joaquim Ros of the Venerable Fr. Josep de Sant Benet, a monk who died in 1723 and who is remembered for his holiness. The entire vault is decorated in a distinctly idealistic style with biblical stories of the Eucharist and scenes of Christmas, Easter and Pentecost by Josep Obiols. The mahogany cupboards along the side walls have marquetry panels –also designed by Josep Obiols– which show saints and other figures linked to Montserrat. The ensemble is extremely beautiful and has especially well-balanced lines.

Josep Obiols painted the Sacristy vaults between 1943 and 1946. They symbolise the liturgical year through the four seasons (from left to right and from top to bottom): winter, with the rising sun representing Christ; spring, with the sacrificial lamb representing the Easter mystery; autumn, with a sun radiant with the face of Christ; and autumn with the scroll of the Evangel and the throne of the Church awaiting the return of Christ.

Washbasin in the Sacristy.

Detail of the panel devoted to Saint Gregory. All the paintings in the Sacristy are by Josep Obiols, and marquetry and furnishing by the Linares brothers.

Sarcophagus of Father Abbot Antoni M. Marcet, by Joan Rebull in 1949.

Overall view of the crypt, built by the architect Josep Folguera in 1951. ▷

The Crypt

A small staircase located in the right-hand side of the Presbytery, at the side of the niche chamber itself, leads down to the Crypt. This sober harmonious barrel-vaulted room was opened in 1951 and designed as the burial place for Abbot Antoni M. Marcet and the monks who gave their lives to Christ in the civil war of 1936-39.

The tombs are placed in two vaults opened in the wall; each has a Carrara marble gravestone engraved with details of the remains contained in the vault. At the back of the room there is a memorial stone to those monks whose remains could not be found. The body of Abbot Marcet lies in a sarcophagus designed by Joan Rebull in the centre of the room behind the altar.

In the side walls are also to be found the tombs and gravestones of Cardinal Anselm M. Albareda, the Abbots Gregori Sunyol, Aureli M. Escarré, Gabriel M. Brasó and Pere Celestí Gusi, all the monks of Montserrat, of Fr. Bernardo López, who was abbot at the Monastery of Our Lady of Montserrat in Manila, and of Bishop Antoni Urbss of Latvia together with his secretary, both of whom died in exile at the Monastery.

Overall view of the upper choir and partial view of the stalls.

The Upper Choir

The Upper Choir, which until 1934 was the only one in the Basilica, is supported by Gothic arches above the chancel of the Church. The most notable feature is the group of neoclassical walnut choir-stalls which replaced the Renaissance choir-stalls carved by Cristóbal de Salamanca in the sixteenth century and burnt during the Napoleonic Wars (apart from a few panels and columns which still remain). The current choir-stalls –a gift to the Monastery from Ferdinand VII– were designed in 1824 by Antoni Cellés, who was the first director of the architecture class at the School of the Noble Arts of the Llotja in Barcelona.

The large nineteenth century polychromatic rose representing the coronation and glorification of Mary is also worthy of note.

The upper choir.

Overall view of the basilica and monastery.

THE MONASTERY

The Community of Monks

The current Montserrat community, consisting of some eighty monks, is dedicated, as in times gone by, to a life of prayer, work and hospitality for the thousands upon thousands of pilgrims who visit the Shrine.

In accordance with the spirit of the Rule of Saint Benedict (a spiritual way of life written in the sixth century but which is sufficiently adaptable to every epoch and every socio-cultural situation), the monks try to live a life of praise and intercession in adoring silence, using the depth of their experience of God and their knowledge of the most profound longings of the human soul in order better to serve men and women everywhere.

Benedictine monasticism is particularly coenobitic (communitarian), and so the monk becomes a brother amongst brothers who help him on his path towards God and enable him to live a life of fraternal love as described in the Gospels.

The neo-Romanesque basilica apses, by Francesc de P. Villar Lozano in 1871, were built to house the Shrine. Behind, we can make out the polygonal apse of the former church, built in Renaissance style.

Pilgrims take part actively in all liturgical celebrations.

Prayer

The monks have always tried to combine solitude with hospitality, two concepts which would appear to be mutually exclusive but which in fact are not. The tension between the two has been fruitful over the years for the monks themselves, the Church and for society. The secular history of the community of Montserrat is eloquent proof of this. Solitude enables the individual to find the light of the Word of God; thus the person gradually moves towards self-acceptance, peace and inner harmony. This occurs above all during the passionate search for God through the liturgy and private prayer.

The liturgy marks the daily rhythm for the monastic day, marking both its beginning and end. The monks come together five times a day to celebrate divine service or the Liturgy of the Hours. In addition to this, there is the celebration of the Eucharist, which is the central event in the day of the Monastery and Shrine. Many pilgrims take part in the monks' liturgy, particularly in the Eucharist and the main hours of divine service.

The monks also set part of the day aside for private prayer and for reading the Word of God or other spiritual works. The ideal situation, as given both by the New Testament and by the Benedictine Rule, is for prayer to God to be as continuous as possible.

Hospitality

The life of the monks in terms of humanity and faith is no different to the basic experience of all men and women because, when all is told, we all live with the same problems around us: problems regarding love, solitude, personal harmony, solidarity, work, use of material goods... and, sometimes, wearied or even weak faith.

The life of faith leads the monk to discover the presence of Christ in another, whoever he or she may be. This means the monk must welcome him or her in a sincere and friendly manner and must feel himself to be the brother of all people.

Work

This openness to solidarity and communion with all manifests itself at Montserrat through various pastoral activities: services at the Basilica, welcoming of groups, retreats and conferences, the provision of lodgings (allowing individuals or groups to spend a few days of reflection and prayer following the rhythm of the monastic community at its most important moments), etc.

In addition to this pastoral work, the monastic chores include the humble tasks required to ensure the good running of the Monastery and the Shrine and some craft work. There are also monks involved in scientific research in various fields including history, theology, translation, biblical studies, liturgy and philosophy. The Monastery has a notable publications service, which publishes numerous books and magazines on science or for circulation on specifically religious as well as cultural themes. The service also puts together records and audiovisual material. Indeed, Montserrat occupies an important position as one of the principal centres of Catalan culture.

Shaped as it is by its uninterrupted history in this place, the community today dedicates itself to the constant search for renewed faith in accordance with the demands of the Church and with its loyalty to the men and women of our times, in its own monastic tradition, in order to continue its service to mankind and especially to the Christians of the country with which it has always been so closely linked.

The Chapter House

This sober, beautifully decorated square-shaped room is the meeting place for the monastic community for important events. The more informal daily meetings are held elsewhere. The Monastery lives as a family and shares both its spiritual as well as material goods, in an attempt to live a Christian life to the full in accordance with the evangelical spirit contained in the Rule of Saint Benedict and under the guidance of an abbot. This fraternal communion involves an element of dialogue, of communication, so that each member of the community is jointly responsible for the running of the

Craft work by the community of monks.

Chapterhouse door.

The Chapterhouse was renovated in 1940 by Santiago Marco, who designed a central space with the furniture forming concentric circles around it. In the centre of the photograph, the Lecture of the Rule of Saint Benedict, on the right, the Abbot's chair and, in the background a painting by Pere Pruna in 1961 depicting Saint Benedict receiving homage for the monks assassinated for their faith during the Civil War.

Mural, also by Pere Pruna, in the Chapterhouse: Father Abbot Marcet presents the two monks who died in the nationalist army to Saint George.

Renaissance door into the Sign Room.

Monastery and helps the abbot in determining the courses of action to be taken.

This room is used for these serious moments of deliberation, judgment and decision making at a community level and also for the monastic conferences which the abbot addresses to the community from time to time.

Near the Chapter House is the Room of the Sign, watched over by a bronze statue of Saint Benedict by Josep Clarà. A sepulchral monument to Abbot Oliba by Enric Monjo and a statue of Abbot García de Cisneros by Francesc Juventeny can be found in this room.

Sign Room: bronze sculpture of Saint Benedict by Josep Clarà in 1946.

Sign Room: cenotaphs of Abbot Oliba, by Enric Monjo in 1946 and, in the background, of Abbot García de Cisneros, the work of Francesc Juventeny in 1947. The sgrafitti in the room were designed and painted by artists from the community of monks in 1946.

Inner cloister of the monastery: lower gallery and tomb of Prior Ramon de Vilaragut (mid-14th century).

The Cloister

The Cloister, constructed in the interior of the Monastery and which connects various outbuildings, was built by Puig i Cadafalch in 1925 in a "Romanesque" style using an unusual combination of stone, brick and wood. The aim of its particularly beautiful lines is to reflect the architectural shapes from the primitive period of the Monastery of Santa Maria.

It is formed by two storeys of brick arches supported by stone columns. All along the walls there is a sizable collection of archeological pieces and gravestones, important for their historical and artistic merit, dating from the tenth to the eighteenth century. The lower floor has a small pavilion with a fountain in the centre, which evokes the great monastic cloisters of Catalonia, and connects to the garden. The wealth of different types of trees and plants in the garden attracts birds, and their singing combined with the sound of the fountain produces a tranquil setting for reflection and peace.

Inner cloister of the monastery: fount in the templete, or shrine, the shrine itself and the lower gallery.

The Refectory

Meals are an important part of fraternal life; the Bible itself emphasises their spiritual nature and teaches that God is present in the communion amongst those eating. Monastic rules therefore give an almost liturgical air to meals, which begin and end in prayer and are conducted in silence. The aim is to feed not only the body but also the spirit through reading which accompanies the meal. The consequence is that refectories in monasteries have a special architectural feel.

The refectory at Montserrat is large and very light and dates from the seventeenth century with some alterations made in 1925 by Puig i Cadafalch. On one side it overlooks the side of the rock itself and on the other, large windows give an excellent view of the mountain. At the presiding end, there is a side apse covered in mosaics showing the Christ in Majesty, inspired by wall paintings in the Pyrenees. At the opposite end, there is a triptych painted in cheerful colours by Josep Obiols, which shows a scene from the life of Saint Benedict. In the centre, there is a stone throne for the reader.

The Library

The library at Montserrat is valuable both for the quality and quantity of its collection of books. The library has approximately 300.000 volumes, among which about 400 incunabulum and about 2.000 manuscripts, among which is one of the eldest known Catalonian texts, from the end of the XII century or of the beginnings of the XIII.

There is documentary evidence of the library at Montserrat as early as the eleventh century. The col-

The monastery refectory, renovated in 1925 by Puig i Cadafalch, who also designed the furnishings.

Central room in the library, renovated by Puig i Cadafalch in 1917; the painting in the background is by Miquel Massot. Below, the Llibre Vermell (Red Book).

lection grew over the years but the Napoleonic Wars, responsible for so much destruction on the mountain, caused the disappearance or dispersal of a large number of its books and archives. Apart from a few pieces which were saved, the current stock was started during the period of reconstruction, particularly during the abbacy of Fr. Antoni M. Marcet. The library has subsequently been enriched by many new additions.

Amongst the manuscripts is the famous fourteenth century *Llibre Vermell* (Red Book) with miniatures from the Montserrat *Scriptorium*. This book is a veritable encyclopedia to medieval Montserrat, its importance being due in part to the collection of the oldest songs and dances in Europe from the pilgrims to the Shrine.

The Hermitage of Sant Iscle, in the monastery garden. This tiny church, which is mentioned in a document dating back to the 9th century, gives us an idea of what the old Chapel of Santa Maria, the origin of the present sanctuary, must have been like.

Terrace of the monastery garden, its floor decorated with a medallion representing the Creation. ▷

Archaeology from the Biblical East, with objects from Mesopotamia, Egypt, Cyprus and the Holy Land.

THE MUSEUM

In 1811 with the Napoleonic Wars, Montserrat lost almost all of its artistic heritage, as we have already seen with the library. In spite of this, a valuable collection of works of art, mostly donated, has been built up since the restoration in 1844. Most of these works are on show in the Museum located below the upper square of the Shrine. This same space, designed by Josep Puig i Cadafalch in 1929, is particularly unusual from an architectural point of view because of the technique used to support the square and the two lower floors.

The Museum is divided into various sections: archeology of the Bible lands, gold-work in the Shrine's Sacristy, paintings by old masters and the extraordinary collection of Catalan paintings and sculptures from the nineteenth and twentieth centuries.

Archeology of the Bible Lands

The archeology of the Bible lands is represented by an important collection of pieces connected to countries in the Bible (Mesopotamia, Egypt, Cyprus and Palestine). The monk Bonaventura Ubach (who died in 1960) gathered these pieces together and began studies of the Bible at Montserrat, which were continued by his followers. In addition to the most important pieces which are on permanent display, the Museum has an alternating show for visitors and scholars of its reserve.

Important pieces from Mesopotamia are the numerous cuneiform tablets in Akkadian, Hittite and Sumerian dating from 3400 BC to 600 BC. There is also a sizeable collection of stone cylinders, with their seals, which provide evidence of the different periods of Mesopotamian history.

From Egypt, there is a collection of ancient funerary objects including a mummy of a twenty-five year old woman from the late period, two sarcophagi, two Canopic vases, statuettes and amulets.

The collection of objects from Palestine includes ceramics from a number of biblical epochs, some dating from 4000 BC; coins, statues of Greek and Caananite gods, Roman and Byzantine glasses, an extensive collection of lamps, etc. The collection of Cypriot ceramics is also interesting, with the earliest pieces dating from the twentieth century BC.

Chalices for wine and water, and another chalice from the communion set donated by the Emperor Ferdinand III in thanks for the protection of Our Lady of Montserrat at battles in the Thirty Years' War. The chalices are made from gold with enamel and scarlet adornment. Behind is the crown that the Catalan people donated to Our Lady of Montserrat (1881).

Gold-work

Gold-work is represented in the Montserrat Museum by a collection of accessories to the liturgy (chalices, patens, cruets, crowns, monstrances, pectoral crosses, etc.) from the fifteenth to the twentieth century, which show the development in techniques and artistic styles. The richly decorated crown and sceptre offered by the Catalans to Our Lady in 1881 when she was proclaimed patron saint of Catalonia are of special importance. There are also the Baroque cruets and chalice of enamelled gold given to Montserrat by Emperor Ferdinand III of Austria in thanks for his victory over Gustavus Adolphus of Italy and the rock crystal reliquary offered to Our Lady in 1605 by the duke of Mantua and Montferrat, Vincenzo de Gonzaga.

Gold and silver work from the 15th-20th centuries.

"The Penitent Magdalene", by El Greco (1531-1614).

"Saint Jerome", by Caravaggio (1573-1619). ▷

"The Tapestry Seller", by Marià Fortuny (1838-1874).

"Port-Marly in Winter", by Alfred Sisley (1839-1899).

"Poor People Waiting for Soup", by Isidre Nonell (1873-1911).

"La Consuelo", by Isidre Nonell (1873-1911).

"The Little One and the Good Companion", by Francesc Gimeno (1858-1927).

"Montmartre Café",
by Santiago Rusiñol
(1861-1931).

"The Blue Patio", by
Santiago Rusiñol
(1861-1931).

"Madeleine. The
Absent" by Ramon
Casas (1865-1932).
The Catalan title of
the painting,
"Madeleine.
L'absenta", plays wit
the word "l'absenta",
which means both
"the absent" and
"absinthe".

"Reflexes", by Joaquim Mir (1873-1940).

"Between Sardana and Sardana", by Xavier Nogués (1873-1940).

"Champs Elysées", by Anglada Camarasa (1872-1959).

"Montserrat from Can Martí Joan (El Bruc)", by Ramon Rogent (1920-1958).

"The Little One Knitting", by Josep Obiols (1894-1967).

"New York", by Joaquim Torres Garcia (1875-1949).

Paintings by Old Masters

This important collection contains old masters from he thirteenth to the eighteenth century including works by Berruguete, Morales, el Greco, Bonfigli, A. de Salerno, Marco Pino, Caravaggio, Luca Giordano and Tiepolo. A large number of these paintings were acquired in Italy between 1914 and 1920 during the time of Abbot Antoni M. Marcet. Catalan and Castilian painting is represented by canvasses from the fifteenth and sixteenth centuries.

Modern Painting and Sculpture

The modern painting and sculpture collection contains a representative selection of work by Catalan artists who were working between the middle of the nineteenth and the middle of the twentieth centuries. The initial core, which went on show in 1982, consists of

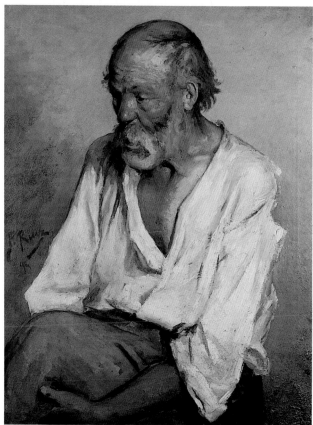

"The Old Fisherman", by Pablo Picasso (1881-1973).

"The Sailor. Neo-Cubist Academy", by Salvador Dalí (1904-1989).

works from the Josep Sala i Ardiz Collection by artists such as Martí Alsina, Vayreda, Gimeno, Rusiñol, Casas, Nonell, Mir, Anglada Camarasa, Picasso and Dalí. Some years later the Xavier Busquets Collection of French Impressionist paintings was added, with works by Monet, Sisley, Degas, Pissarro, Rouault and Poliakoff. Works by other artists such as Singer Sargent, Sorolla, Julio Romero de Torres and Zuloaga complete this section of the museum. The artists represented mean that the Museum of Montserrat has one of the best collections of Catalan *Modernista* and French Impressionist painting in Catalonia.

"Nigra sum": Iconography of Saint Mary of Montserrat

The Museum also has a permanent exhibition on the

"Our Lady of Montserrat", by Juan A. Ricci (1600-1681).

history of the Image of Our Lady of Montserrat to help pilgrims and visitors understand the historical evolution of the Image of Saint Mary that is venerated at Montserrat. This exhibition is entitled Nigra sum meaning "I am a black woman" in reference to the text in the book of the Song of Songs 1, 5 which says "I am black, but comely", words which perfectly suit the Image of Our Lady of Montserrat in the physical sense

as well as in the symbolic or theological sense. The exhibition shows the developments in the rich iconography over the course of various epochs, from the twelfth century to 1947 when the Image was installed on the throne in the Niche. There are pieces of sculpture, paintings (Joan A. Ricci, c.1639; Olga Sacharoff, 1947, and others), drawings, engravings (some from 1499), medals, etc.

The path to the Holy Cave is decorated with 15 sculptures forming the Monumental Rosary. The sculpture in the photograph is that of the Resurrection of Christ and was first unveiled in 1916. The work was designed by Gaudí, whilst the sculptures of Christ Resuscitated and the Angel of the Resurrection are by Josep Llimona, and the Group of the Maries, by Dionís Renart.

The Holy Cave.

THE VIA CRUCIS

The Way of the Cross begins a little beyond the Plaça Abat Oliba behind the Font del Portal (the Fountain of the Portal) and continues on to the Chapel of Our Lady of Sorrows, close to the Sant Miquel path. The route is gentle and beautifully shaded and is one of the prettiest places in the area, offering a pleasant panorama of the Shrine.

Fourteen monuments corresponding to the Stations of the Cross were erected between 1904 and 1919 but were completely destroyed in the 1936 war. Some new Stations have been set up using sculptures by Margarida Sans Jordi and Francesc Juventeny; the remaining Stations will be by Domènec Fita using a particularly stylised design.

LA SANTA COVA

The path which leads to the Santa Cova (Holy Cave) starts near the cable car and continues for about one and a half kilometres along a route established in the seventeenth century. Financial support from the faithful contributed to the fifteen sculptural groups corresponding to the fifteen Mysteries of the Rosary set up along the route. Gaudí, Puig i Cadafalch, Josep Llimona, the Vallmitjana brothers and others all worked on these pieces of sculpture.

Almost hanging from the rock at the end of the route is the Chapel where legend has it that the Image of Our Lady of Montserrat was found. The current building is by and large the same as the seventeenth century building which was rebuilt twice, firstly because of the damage suffered in the Napoleonic Wars in 1811 and later after damage caused by the fire in 1994 and the collapse of the dome in September 1995. There are some outbuildings used as a dwelling by the monk who welcomes pilgrims there and a charming small cloister. The simple small chapel, built to the design of a Greek cross and dome, backs onto a grotto in the mountain, where there is a stylised reproduction of the authentic Image in the Basilica. The entire place is peaceful and solitary.

"ELS DEGOTALLS" PATH

This 45-minute walk begins on the Monistrol road, passing by the self-service café. Before taking the

"Els Degotalls" path.

path, a pause on the terraces of the self-service café or restaurant allows us to admire a magnificent panoramic view over the Llobregat Valley. On a clear day, we can also make out Mount Tibidabo and the sea to the east and the Pyrenees to the north. The beginning of the path is marked by a monument to Jacint Verdaguer, erected in 1931. The route, adorned by other monuments and wall tiles evoking different Marian advocations, ends at "Els Degotalls", a rock formation from which water once used to spring.

HERMITAGES

There are some 15 chapels, former hermitages, dotted over Mount Montserrat, including that at the Holy Cave. Formerly subject to the dioceses of Barcelona or Vic, they were all abandoned when the hermits were forced to flee before the French invasion in 1811. Though they were later rebuilt, few were inhabited once more and most were finally abandoned in 1822, after which the buildings began to deteriorate. All that remains now, in some cases, are the walls.

Sant Joan funicular railway.

The **Hermitage of Sant Joan** is one of the most accessible from the Sanctuary. To reach it, we take the funicular railway of the same name. From the station at the top, we can enjoy splendid views of the monastery. A pleasant path starts out at this point, a twenty-minute walk to the chapel, which was built into the rock. In its place today is a cave and several exquisitely-carved stone benches. Next, we see a grille and a short tunnel leading to the former **Hermitage of Sant Onofre**, which also perches on the rocks. Here we can see the cistern, excavated into the very stone. The two hermitages were once separated by a wall, built to preserve the solitude demanded by meditation.

The **Hermitage of Sant Miquel** is also easily accessible. It is reached by a broad path that starts out in Plaça Abat Oliba and follows the first stretch of the old Collbató road, which was the most important in medieval Montserrat, taken by hosts of pilgrims of all social conditions. Though documented

The Chapel of Sant Miquel and the viewpoint nearby.

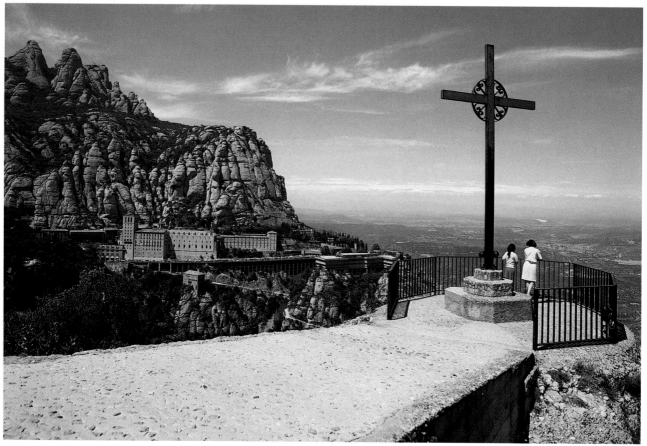

The old cable car that once took passengers up to the peak of Sant Jeroni. Hermitages of Sant Dimes, La Santa Creu and La Santíssima Trinitat.

as far back as the 10th century, the present building is a much later reconstruction, inaugurated in 1870. Just 100 metres or so to the left of the chapel, a path leads to a viewpoint over a precipice over 200 metres high, commanding magnificent views of the Llobregat Valley below and the Pyrenees in the background.

To visit the **Hermitage of Sant Jeroni**, we take a path that starts at the upper station on the Sant Joan funicular railway line. Taking around an hour and a half,

this is one of the most beautiful walks in Montserrat Natural Park, as it culminates at the peak of Sant Jeroni, the highest point in the mountain (1,236 m). Beside the funicular railway station is a path leading through leafy woods to the northwest. Along the way, enjoying magnificent views, we can make out on the other side of the valley, from right to left, the hermitages of Sant Dimes, La Santa Creu, La Santíssima Trinitat and Sant Benet.

Before the **Hermitage of Sant Dimes** was built, a for-

Hermitages of Sant Salvador and Santa Anna.

building built later, and now used as a mountain refuge.

Finally, the path leads to the chapel built to replace the **Hermitage of Sant Jeroni**, which stood on the site of the viewpoint. Beside it, steps lead up to the peak of Sant Jeroni, where a large table enables visitors to identify the surrounding relief points, ranging from the Pyrenees to Els Ports mountains and Majorca.

All that remains of the **Hermitage of Sant Jaume** are the wall foundations, now half-hidden amongst the vegetation. The hermitage stands on a rock known as "Gorra Marinera", and which commands fine views of the monastery. From here, the hermit could hear the church organ and monks' choir at song and prayer.

Near this "Gorra Marinera" rock stands the **Hermitage of Santa Magdalena**, of which only remains of walls and cisterns are conserved. The other hermitages on Montserrat have suffered similar neglect: the **Hermitage of Santa Caterina** (situated below a rock at the springs of the Santa Caterina mountain torrent, built in a grotto that now serves as a refuge for climbers and hikers); the **Hermitage of Sant Antoni** (over the "Paret dels Diables", near "Cavall Bernat"); the **Hermitage of Sant Salvador** (at the foot of the rock known as "L'Elefant"); and the **Hermitage of Santa Anna** (by the María mountain torrent, beside the crossroads of the paths leading to the other chapels, not far from the monastery, for which reason this was where the hermits came twice a week to hear mass).

SANTA CECÍLIA

The former Monastery of Santa Cecília stood some four kilometres from that of Montserrat, on the road to Can Maçana. The church, simple and austere, basically that same as that originally built in the 10th century, is one of the purest examples of early Catalan Romanesque art. The three apses, with Lombard arches, correspond to the nave and two aisles in the interior, with hammer-carved stone walls that were originally whitewashed. The building is harmoniously integrated into the landscape, forming a beautiful site. The monastery was founded between 942 and 945 by Abbot Cesari. The community was never large, and the monastery was finally merged with that of Montserrat in 1539. Today, Santa Cecília houses a mountain refuge.

tification stood here, built at the command of King Peter of Aragon. Later, some 30 bandoleers made this their stronghold, robbing pilgrims until they were finally driven off by a group of countrymen. The original building was left in ruins and the chapel was built, though it now houses a weather station.

Much of the **Hermitage of La Santa Creu** has been conserved, along with the two cisterns, still in use. This is one of the few hermitages inhabited in modern times, its last occupant being Father Basilio, who died at the age of 78 on 23 December 2003.

All that remains of the **Hermitage of La Santíssima Trinitat** are remains of some of the walls, the cistern and the Chapel of El Sant Crist. More rooms were added to the hermitage in the 17th century as, along with the Hermitage of Sant Dimes, it had direct access to the monastery via a staircase with 660 steps.

The **Hermitage of Sant Benet** was built in 1536 to shorten the distance between the two hermitages. All that now remains, however, is a chapel-shaped

Apse in the former Monastery of Santa Cecília.

Dancing sardanes in Abat Oliba square.

THE POPULAR ASPECT OF MONTSERRAT

Montserrat has many features, one of which is its extraordinary popularity. Many Catalans make a customary annual visit, either individually or with their family. There are frequent weddings, birthdays, public festivals and other similar events. Some families or groups spend Easter in its characteristic setting or they come for a few days of relaxation and brotherhood during the summer holidays. Some parishes organise pilgrimages, during which time Montserrat takes on a festive air and offers a renewal of Christian life according to a pastoral plan proposed each year by the Shrine. Many cultural and religious groups include a visit to the Shrine as part of their activities and leave flags, emblems or other offerings as evidence of their stay.

It is frequently even the setting for cultural events or popular festivals. On certain occasions, people express their joy by dancing the sardana, the traditional dance of Catalonia.

However, these events have been influenced by the social changes that are characteristic of our age, taking on new forms. Tourism has had a particularly strong influence on the appearance of Montserrat in recent years, particularly in spring and summer when large groups of visitors effectively invade the Shrine. Many visitors, apart from being able to buy records, books and other souvenirs from their visit to Montserrat in the spacious premises located in front of the train station, deepen their knowledge of what is the Monastery from the inside and on the values it wants to promote, thanks to a thematic space –"Montserrat portes endins" (Montserrat behind closed doors)– which explains how is the monastic life in Montserrat.

Montserrat is a natural phenomenon which, in addition to its principal religious function, has become a cultural centre, a popular place for excursions and tourist visits and an attractive location for many climbers, all facilitated by easy means of transport. All of this contributes to increasing the interest which this holy, beautiful mountain has always aroused far and wide throughout Catalonia.

VIROLAI

Rosa d'abril, Morena de la serra
de Montserrat Estel,
il·lumineu la catalana terra,
guieu-nos cap al cel.

Amb serra d'or els angelets serraren
eixos turons per fer-vos un palau;
Reina del Cel que els serafins baixaren
deu-nos abric dins vostre mantell blau.

Alba naixent d'estrelles coronada,
Ciutat de Déu que somnià David,
a vostres peus la lluna s'és posada,
el sol sos raigs us dóna per vestit.

Dels catalans sempre sereu Princesa,
dels espanyols l'Estrella d'Orient,
sigueu pels bons pilar de fortalesa,
pels pecadors el port de salvament.

Doneu consol a qui la pàtria enyora
sens veure mai els cims de Montserrat;
en terra i mar oïu a qui us implora,
torneu a Déu els cors que l'han deixat.

Mística Font de l'aigua de la vida,
rageu del Cel al cor de mon país,
dons i virtuts deixeu-li per florida;
feu-ne, si us plau, el vostre paradís.

Ditxosos ulls, Maria, els que us vegen,
ditxós el cor que s'obre a la vostra llum;
Rosa del Cel que els Serafins voltegen,
a ma oració doneu vostre perfum.

Cedre gentil del Líbano corona,
Arbre d'encens, Palmera de Sion,
el fruit sagrat que vostre amor ens dóna,
és Jesucrist, el Redemptor del món.

Amb vostre nom comença nostra història
i és Montserrat el nostre Sinaí;
siguin per tots l'escala de la glòria
eixos penyals coberts de romaní.

JACINT VERDAGUER

Els Flautats

Cavall Bernat

St. Jeroni

Les Talaies

Ecos

Els Aurons

Pla de la Trinitat

La Mòmia

L'Elefant

Roca de St. Salvador

Els Flautats

Coll de Porc
El Novici
El Frare Gros
El Bastó del Frare
El Lloro
El Bisbe
La Nina
La Boleta Foradada
Agulla del Centenar
El Queixal
El Gendarme
La Boleta del Portell Estret
Coll de les Agulles
L'Escorpí
La Torta
L'Agulla dels Ossos
L'Arbret
La Bandereta

Barretines
Cavall Bernat
Paret dels Diables
Serrat del Patriarca
Paret del Mirador del Moro
Coll de Porc
Frares

La Cadireta · La Foradada · L'Escorpí · La Torta · La Boteruda del Grà · La Miranda dels Ossos · Agulla de l'Arbret

Services at the Sanctuary
1. Our Lady of Montserrat
2. Basilica
3. Pastoral Coordination Centre
4. Museum of Montserrat
5. "Montserrat Portes Endins" Audiovisual Space

Bars and Restaurants
6. Restaurant Abat Cisneros

7. Mirador dels Apòstols
   Bar del Mirador
   Self-Service
   Restaurant de Montserrat
8. La Cafeteria
9. Bar de la Plaça

Accommodation
10. Hotel Abat Cisneros ★★★
11. Cells (apartments)
12. Cells Reception

13. La Botiga (shops)
14. Cakes and Pastries
15. Supermarket

Transport
16. Overhead railway
17. Sant Joan funicular railway
18. Santa Cova funicular railway
19. Rack railway

Information · **Children** · **WC** · **Picnic ar** · **Public telephone** · **Panoram**

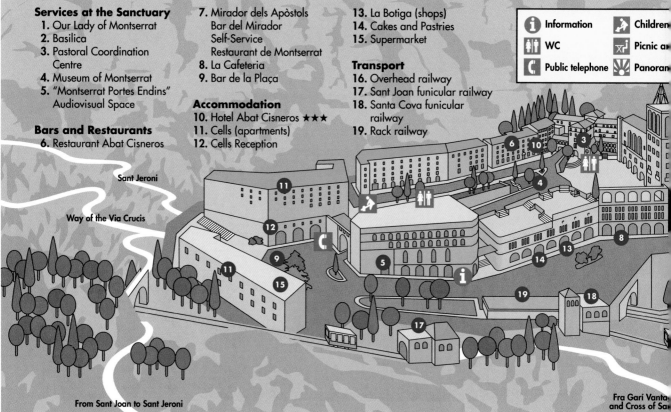

Sant Jeroni

Way of the Via Crucis

From Sant Joan to Sant Jeroni

Fra Garí Vanta and Cross of Sa

La Saca
La Banderata
Ninet
La Figuereta
El Senatxo
El Sabre
L'Agulla del Capdemunt
Les Savines

"Els Degotalls" and the "Magnificant" path

Way of la Santa Cova

— Rack train
HHHH FGC Line

**ACCESSES TO THE
MONTSERRAT SANCTUARY**

Sant Joan
funicular railway
**Montserrat
Station**
Santa Cova
funicular railway
Overheat railway
of Montserrat
Llobregat river
← Barcelona
Manresa →
**Monistrol-Vila
Station**

Montserrat-Aeri Station
**Monistrol-Enllaç
Station**

103

CONTENTS

A SURPRISING WORLD 3

THE MONASTERY IS BORN 24

HISTORICAL BACKGROUND.................25

A LAND OF FANTASY:
THE NATURAL PARK.................................30

THE "MORENETA" 32

THE CHOIR 34

THE BASILICA...36
The Atrium...36
The Church..42
The Niche 56
The New Sacristy.......................................62
The Crypt 64
The Upper Choir 66

THE MONASTERY 68
The Community of Monks 68
Prayer 70
Hospitality..70
Work 71
The Chapter House...................................71

The Cloister 74
The Refectory 76
The Library 76

THE MUSEUM 80
Archeology of the Bible Lands................80
Gold-work...81
Paintings by Old Masters 89
Modern Painting and Sculpture 89
"Nigra sum": Iconography of Saint Mary of
Montserrat 90

THE VIA CRUCIS 92

LA SANTA COVA.......................................92

"ELS DEGOTALLS" PATH 92

HERMITAGES 93

SANTA CECÍLIA 96

THE POPULAR ASPECT OF MONTSERRAT.........98

VIROLAI 99

MAP OF MONTSERRAT 102

EDITORIAL ESCUDO DE ORO, S.A.
Palaudàries, 26 - 08004 Barcelona
Tel: 93 230 86 10 - E-mail: editorial@eoro.com

I.S.B.N. 84-378-1845-1
Printed by FISA - Escudo de Oro, S.A.
Legal Dep. B. 19810-2004

Protegemos el bosque; papel procedente de cultivos forestales controlados
Wir schützen den Wald. Papier aus kontrollierten Forsten.
We protect our forests. The paper used comes from controlled forestry plantations
Nous sauvegardons la forêt: papier provenant de cultures forestières contrôlées